Hailee Oman · Gustyawan

My **SLOTH** and the very **CONTAGIOUS** case of the **YAWNS**

Warning!

This book contains content that is extremely contagious and may produce YAWNS without warning!

Reader Discretion Advised

This is my sloth!
It's normal for her to move very slooooowwwly,
but something is different about her!

She can't stop YAWNING!

YAWWWWWWWWWWN!

She YAWNS no matter what I do!

She **YAWNS** when I brush her hair...

She **YAWNS** when she eats...

She YAWNS when I give her a bubble bath...

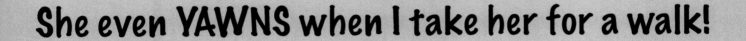
She even YAWNS when I take her for a walk!

She can't stop YAWNING!

YAWWWWWWWWWWN!

Oh no!

I hope she doesn't have a case of the YAWNS!

I hear they are extremely CONTAGIOUS!

I'm going to help her get into bed!
Maybe that will make her feel better!

My poor sloth!
Her eyes look SOOOOO heavy!

She looks SOOOOO sleepy!

She is SOOOOO comfy in her nice, warm, soft, bed!

She's falling asleep!

My sloth fell asleep!

Wow!
Her YAWNS have completely disappeared!

YAWWWWWWWWWWWN!

I'm suddenly SOOOO sleepy!
My eyes are SOOOOOOO heavy!

I can't stop YAWNING!

Oh no!

I'm starting to YAWN, just like my sloth!

I think I may have also caught a case of the YAWNS!

Hmmmm, I wonder if the YAWNS will go away if I get ready for bed and try to sleep!

These **YAWNS** are SOOOO contagious!

I hope **YOU** don't catch them
while you read this book!

I'm going to get into my warmest, softest, snuggliest, jammies!

I hope I can fall asleep fast, so my YAWNS go away!

YAWWWWWWWWWWN!

My sloth is still sleeping!

Her YAWNS haven't returned!
I hope I don't wake her up!

SHHHHHHHHHHH!

I'm SOOOOO warm and comfy in my soft bed!

I am SOOOOO tired!

I can hardly keep my eyes open!

Just remember!

If you catch a contagious case of the YAWNS, getting ready for bed and going to sleep should do the trick!

Good Night!

WAIT!

Did you or your little one catch a contagious case of the Yawns?

Please warn others by leaving a review!

Thank You!

JOIN THE CLUB!

IT'S FUN, AND IT'S FREE!

VISIT
WWW.LITTLELEAFBOOKCLUB.COM

About the Author

Hi Readers!
My name is Hailee Oman, and I LOVE publishing books with sentiment and humor!
I find that when both the child AND parent are having a good time,
they will read longer, and build a love for reading!

You will always find humor, along with a sentimental or humorous message to
parents and caregivers in ALL of my books!

I am very passionate about giving back and helping underserved communities!
This is why I hope to grow Little Leaf Book Club into a non profit organization that
will provide books to kids all over the world who cannot afford them!

By sharing my books, joining Little Leaf Book Club, and leaving a review on
Amazon, you can help me give back to these communities!

Please take a moment to check out my bookstore at www.littleleafbookclub.com
for deals, future giveaways, free eBooks, products, updates and more!

I genuinely thank you!

-Hailee Oman
www.littleleafbookclub.com

Scan Me

Made in the USA
Middletown, DE
08 December 2022

17744339R00031